ANNABEL KARMEL

Cook It Together

Find out what we're making on page 16.

LONDON, NEW YORK,
MELBOURNE, MUNICH, and DELHI

Designed by Rachael Foster
Edited by Penny Smith
Design assistance and illustrations
Clémence de Molliens
Photography Dave King
Food stylist Valerie Berry

Production editor Siu Chan
Jacket editor Mariza O'Keefe
Publishing manager Bridget Giles

First published in Great Britain in 2009 by
Dorling Kindersley Limited,
80 Strand, London, WC2R 0RL

Copyright © 2009 Dorling Kindersley Limited
A Penguin Company

This edition published 2009 for Index Books Ltd

2 4 6 8 10 9 7 5 3
WD185 – 10/08

A CIP catalogue record for this book is available
from the British Library

ISBN: 978-1-40534-425-8

Printed and bound by Toppan, China

Discover more at
www.dk.com

Contents

⚠ *All the recipes in this book are for adults and children to cook together, and when this symbol appears extra care should be taken.*

Staying cosy indoors and cooking delicious homemade food together is a wonderful way to enjoy your day. So I've created some easy, yet very tasty, step-by-step recipes you and your child will love making together.

Throughout this book, I've focused on 10 important ingredients – tomatoes, sweetcorn, potatoes, rice, bananas, strawberries, apples, honey, chocolate, and yoghurt. You'll see how they are grown or made, and discover fun facts about them.

And I've used lots of lovely herbs and spices to flavour my recipes. Find out about them over the page.

Cooking is great for boosting your child's confidence and inspiring creativity. And you never know, you might ignite a passion for cookery in your little ones that goes way beyond licking the spoon: from child cook to Michelin Star chef maybe!

Pop on your pinnies, roll up your sleeves, and get stuck in!

Annabel Karmel

Fantastic Flavours

Herbs and spices are a wonderful way to add flavour and colour to dishes. Here are the ones I've used in recipes in this book.

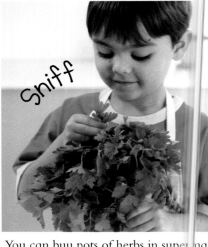

Sniff

Keeping fresh
Keep dried herbs and spices fresh by storing them in airtight containers in a cool, dark place.

You can buy pots of herbs in supermarkets. They have a lovely colour and smell.

cinnamon
ground cinnamon

cinnamon sticks

This spice is made from the bark of the cinnamon tree, and you buy it as short sticks or powder.

vanilla
vanilla pods

vanilla extract

Vanilla comes from the pod of the vanilla orchid. Use the seeds inside whole pods or vanilla extract.

paprika

This is a fine red spice made from sweet pepper pods. Paprika has a mildly hot flavour.

thyme

A little thyme adds gorgeous flavour to a dish.

mint

Strong and fresh tasting, mint is lovely served with something cooling, such as yoghurt.

lemon grass

dill
Dill has a light aniseed flavour.

basil

Basil is lovely with tomatoes.

chives

Chives are from the onion family.

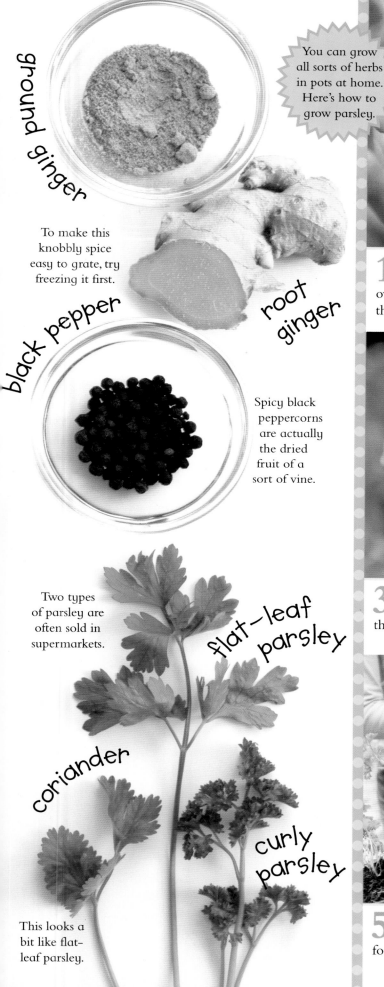

ground ginger

root ginger

To make this knobbly spice easy to grate, try freezing it first.

black pepper

Spicy black peppercorns are actually the dried fruit of a sort of vine.

Two types of parsley are often sold in supermarkets.

flat-leaf parsley

coriander

curly parsley

This looks a bit like flat-leaf parsley.

You can grow all sorts of herbs in pots at home. Here's how to grow parsley.

Grow your own parsley

1 First fill a pot with rich potting compost. Sprinkle over about 5 seeds and cover them with a light layer of soil.

2 Water your seeds well. Keep them on a sunny windowsill. It will take around 8 weeks for them to grow.

3 When the plants are about 8 cm (3 in) tall, carefully dig them out of their first pot...

4 ... and plant them in their own individual pots. You can keep them outside now.

5 Water your parsley regularly and feed it with liquid plant food once a month.

6 When it is dark green and bushy, snip off bits to use in your cooking.

Tomatoes are planted in a freshly ploughed field. They need sunshine and plenty of water to grow.

On this plant, unripe tomatoes are yellow. They turn orange, then ripe red.

In cooler climates, tomatoes are grown under cover. They are harvested as soon as they are ripe.

Tomatoes

Tomatoes are actually a fruit, not a vegetable. They are fantastically useful and go in all sorts of things from bottles of tomato ketchup to salads and soups.

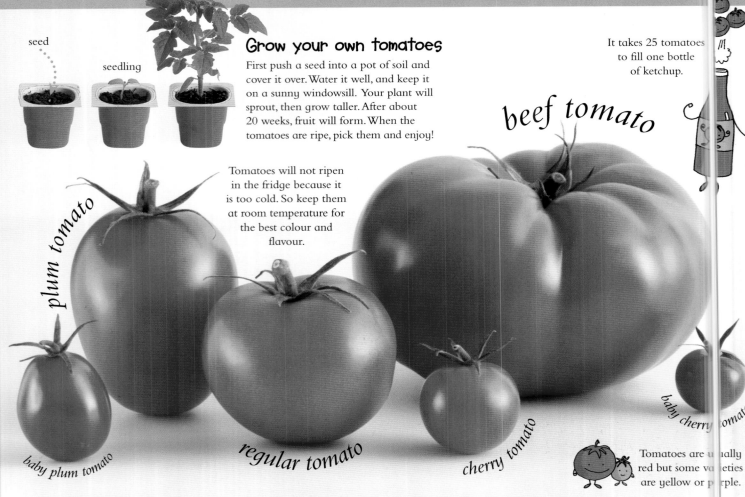

seed

seedling

Grow your own tomatoes

First push a seed into a pot of soil and cover it over. Water it well, and keep it on a sunny windowsill. Your plant will sprout, then grow taller. After about 20 weeks, fruit will form. When the tomatoes are ripe, pick them and enjoy!

It takes 25 tomatoes to fill one bottle of ketchup.

beef tomato

Tomatoes will not ripen in the fridge because it is too cold. So keep them at room temperature for the best colour and flavour.

plum tomato

baby plum tomato

regular tomato

cherry tomato

baby cherry tomato

Tomatoes are usually red but some varieties are yellow or purple.

Tomatoes can be as small as a grape, as big as a melon, or any size in between.

Tomato Bruschetta

Bruschetta is Italian for toast, and these warm, juicy tomatoes on toast make a lovely lunch or light supper.

You will need:
240 g (9 oz) cherry tomatoes
(that's about 20)
1 tbsp olive oil
4 small sprigs thyme
salt and pepper
4 slices country-style bread
1 clove garlic
basil leaves
Parmesan

Halve

Scatter

Rub

1 Preheat the oven to 200°C/400°F/ Gas 6. Line a baking sheet with baking parchment. Halve the tomatoes and sit them on the baking sheet.

2 Drizzle over 1 tsp of the olive oil and scatter over the thyme leaves. Season with salt and pepper. Bake the tomatoes for 6–8 minutes until soft.

3 Toast the bread and let it cool a little. Cut the garlic in half and rub it over one side of the toast. Trickle on the remaining olive oil.

Makes 4

cherry tomatoes

4 Carefully spoon the tomatoes onto the toast and scatter over the basil leaves. Use a potato peeler to shave a few flakes of Parmesan on top. Serve warm.

Tomato Soup

This is tomato soup with a smile. It makes a delicious light meal when served with crispy bread or breadsticks.

Serves 4

You will need:

1 small red onion
½ small red pepper
½ carrot
1 clove garlic
1 tbsp olive oil
400 g (14 oz) tin chopped tomatoes
3 tbsp tomato puree
3 tbsp tomato ketchup
2 tbsp caster sugar
small bunch fresh thyme leaves
250 ml (8 fl oz) vegetable stock
salt and pepper
4 tbsp double cream
basil leaves, olive slices, whipped
   cream, to serve

Chop

1 First prepare the vegetables: chop the onion and dice the pepper.

Crush

2 Peel the carrot, then grate it on the roughest side of the grater. Crush the garlic.

3 Heat the oil, add the onion, pepper, and carrot, and cook for 5 minutes. Pour in the tinned tomatoes, and add the tomato puree, tomato ketchup, garlic, sugar, thyme, and stock. Simmer for 30 minutes.

Pour

☆ **Annabel's Tip**
Use thyme leaves, not stalk. Somewhere around 10 leaves is about right.

4 Season the mixture with salt and pepper. Then blend the soup until it's smooth. Stir in the 4 tbsp cream and serve.

Blend

☆ Annabel's Tip
To decorate your soup with funny faces, make eyes from basil leaves and olive slices, then pipe on the rest of the faces using whipped cream. And remember, the cooler the soup, the longer your faces will stay put!

Sweetcorn plants can reach up to 3½ m (12 ft) tall – so you could get lost in a field of them!

ears of corn ready for picking

Sweetcorn

Sweetcorn is a high-energy food that is healthy and delicious. You can buy it fresh, still wrapped in its green leaves, or tinned, or frozen, or dried. The best fresh corn has plump kernels full of sweet, milky juice.

Sweetcorn is a kind of maize. It grows in warm places. Most of the world's sweetcorn comes from the US.

corn on the cob

kernels

There are about 600–800 kernels on an average corn on the cob.

Count the rows on a piece of sweetcorn. How many are there? The answer is always an even number.

silks

The tufty bits on an ear of corn are called silks. They turn brown at the ends when the corn is ready to pick.

The ear is covered by tightly wrapped leaves called the husk.

These dried corn kernels are used to make popcorn.

popping corn

POP!

From this...

...to this.

mini sweetcorn

Put the dried corn kernels in a pan with a little oil and they will pop into POPCORN!

Sweetcorn and Chicken Pasta Salad

Sweetcorn, chicken, and noodles are often seen together in soups, but here is something similar as a yummy salad.

Serves 4

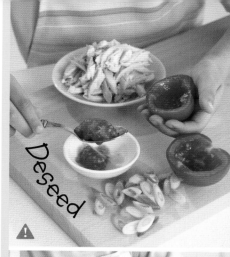

Deseed

1 Cook the pasta according to the packet instructions. Rinse with cold water. Then shred the chicken, slice the spring onions, deseed and chop the tomato.

Snip

2 Put the mayonnaise, yoghurt, and lemon juice in a large bowl. Snip in the dill, season with salt and pepper, and then stir everything together.

Tip

3 Now tip the cold pasta, chicken, spring onions, chopped tomato, and sweetcorn onto the mayonnaise mixture.

4 Mix all the ingredients together and serve.

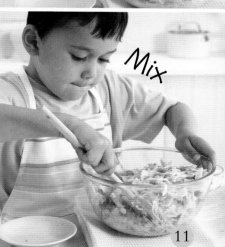

Mix

11

Sweetcorn Fritters

These are popular in southern American states and are great eaten with friends and family. For big parties, simply double the quantities.

You will need:

30 g (1 oz) flour
1 tsp baking powder
pinch of salt
1 egg
1 tbsp maple syrup
2 tbsp milk
198 g (7 oz) tin sweetcorn
2 spring onions, chopped
1–2 tbsp sunflower oil
tomatoes and basil, to serve

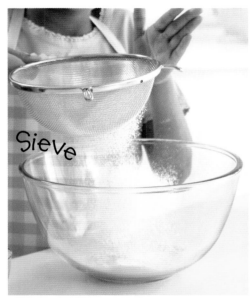

Sieve

1 First sieve the flour, baking powder, and pinch of salt into a large bowl.

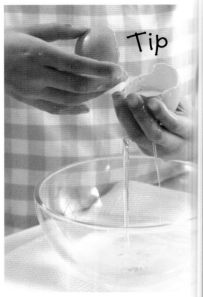

Tip

2 Separate the egg by tipping the yolk from one half of the shell to the other. Let the egg white fall into one bowl. Drop the yolk into another.

Pour

3 Add the maple syrup and milk to the egg yolk and whisk together. Pour this mixture over the flour. Stir everything together to make a batter.

Whisk

4 Then whisk the egg white until it forms stiff peaks. Be careful not to overwhisk or it will go flat.

Fold

5 Use a spatula to fold the egg white into the flour mixture – carefully stirring around the side of the bowl and across the middle.

Tip

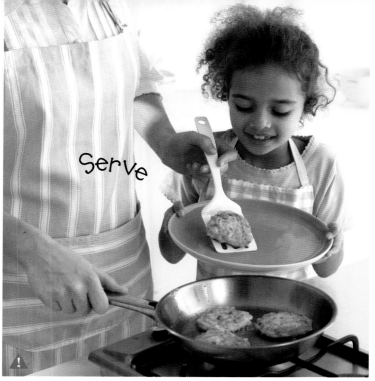

Serve

6 Next tip the tinned sweetcorn and chopped spring onions into the batter mixture. Fold them in – be as light as you can here.

7 Heat the oil, drop in tablespoons of the batter and cook for 1-2 minutes until the undersides are golden. Flip over, cook the other sides, then serve.

*These fritters are delicious served with a **tomato** and **basil salad**.*

juicy pieces of corn

Makes
8–10

✩**Annabel's Tip**
Try dishing up these fritters for breakfast. Simply serve them with chopped banana and extra maple syrup.

To make the field ready for planting, the farmer ploughs the soil and lifts out any stones. Then he uses a potato-planting machine to drop seed potatoes into the soil and cover them over.

Around 2-6 weeks after planting, the shoots begin to push out of the soil. Under the ground, potatoes (called tubers) form. Once the plants flower, young new potatoes can be harvested.

At the end of the summer, mature potatoes are ready to be dug up. These can be stored for months – but make sure you keep them in the dark as light makes them turn green.

Potatoes

People have been growing potatoes for centuries. And whatever their colour – white, brown, yellow, purple, red, or blue – potatoes are a delicious and filling addition to any meal.

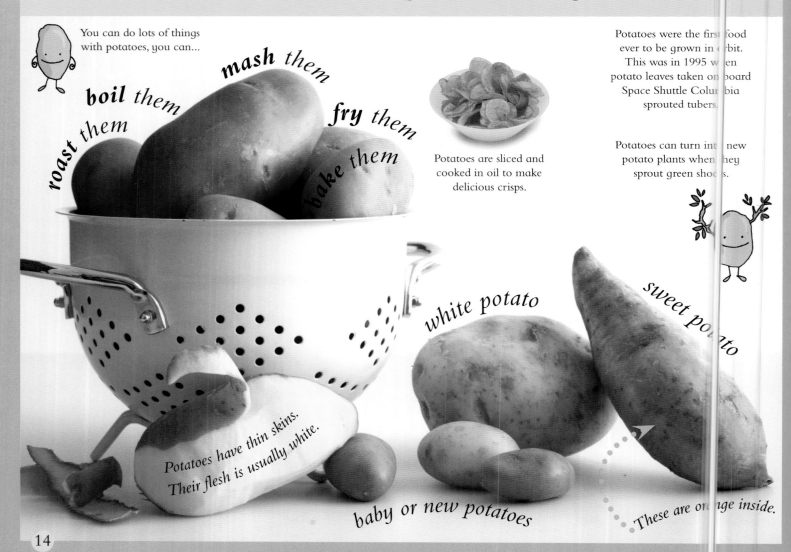

You can do lots of things with potatoes, you can...

roast them
boil them
mash them
fry them
bake them

Potatoes are sliced and cooked in oil to make delicious crisps.

Potatoes were the first food ever to be grown in orbit. This was in 1995 when potato leaves taken on board Space Shuttle Columbia sprouted tubers.

Potatoes can turn into new potato plants when they sprout green shoots.

white potato

sweet potato

Potatoes have thin skins. Their flesh is usually white.

baby or new potatoes

These are orange inside.

Potato Wedges

Serves 4

These wedges are a healthy and easy alternative to chips, but just as delicious. You can make them spicy by adding paprika or fajita seasoning.

You will need:

2 large potatoes
1 tbsp olive oil
salt and pepper
½ tsp paprika or fajita
seasoning (optional)

Soured cream dip

Mix together 3 tbsp soured cream, 1 tbsp mayonnaise, 2 tsp milk, 2 tsp snipped chives, and ½ crushed clove garlic. Season with salt and pepper and serve with the wedges.

Serve with a soured cream and chive dip.

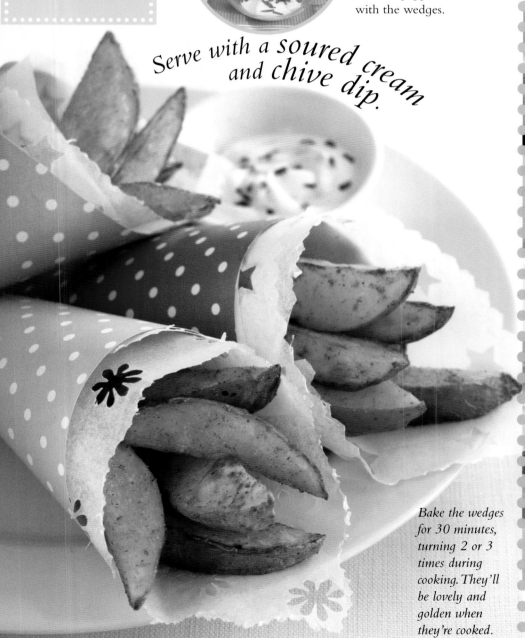

Bake the wedges for 30 minutes, turning 2 or 3 times during cooking. They'll be lovely and golden when they're cooked.

Cut

1 Preheat the oven to 200°C/ 400°F/Gas 6. Cut each potato lengthways into thick wedges.

Mix

2 Put the oil, salt and pepper into a bowl. Add the paprika or fajita seasoning, if using. Then add the potatoes and mix thoroughly.

Bake

3 Lay the wedges on a baking sheet lined with parchment.

Potato Soufflés

Makes 4

The word *soufflé* comes from the French *souffler*, which means "to puff". When you see these come out of the oven, you'll understand why!

You will need:

- 30 g (1 oz) butter,
  plus extra for greasing
- 85 g (3 oz) mature Cheddar
- 30 g (1 oz) Parmesan
- small bunch chives
- 2 eggs
- 1 large baking potato, cooked
- 6 tbsp milk
- pepper

Cook your potato

You can microwave your potato for 7–8 minutes. Alternatively, boil it whole and unpeeled for 35 minutes or until tender. Peel when cool.

☆Annabel's Tip

Soufflés don't stay risen for very long, so it is best to get everyone ready to eat before you take them out of the oven. Serve straight away (though be careful as they will be hot!).

Butter

1 Preheat the oven to 220°C/450°F/ Gas 7 and put a baking sheet in the oven to heat up. Then generously butter 4 ramekin dishes.

Grate

2 Grate the Cheddar and Parmesan cheeses. Snip the chives into small pieces (you should have about 2 tsp). Then separate the eggs.

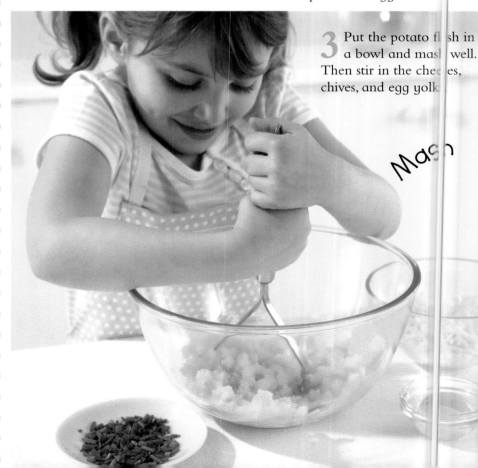

3 Put the potato flesh in a bowl and mash well. Then stir in the cheeses, chives, and egg yolks.

Mash

Pour

Fill

6 Fill the prepared ramekins with the mixture. Put the ramekins on the hot baking sheet and bake for 15-17 minutes until puffed and golden.

4 Warm the milk and butter in a pan, then pour this over the potato mixture and stir everything together. Season with pepper (the Parmesan is already quite salty).

Whisk

5 Whisk the egg whites to floppy peaks. Next gently fold the egg whites into the potato mixture.

Rice is grown in flooded meadows called paddy fields. The water helps to keep away weeds.

After about 4 months, rice is ready for harvesting. It is picked by hand or combine harvester.

This field has been partly harvested. The hard rice grains are carried away in sacks.

Rice

Rice is an excellent store-cupboard ingredient because it keeps for ages and has a mild flavour that goes with lots of food. A little rice goes a long way – when you cook it, it swells to three times its original size.

There are around 40,000 types of rice, although only a small number of them are sold in our supermarkets.

Rice has two outer layers, like coats. On the outside is the hull, under this is the bran, and under this a grain of white rice.

• Rice is the main food for half the people in the world – in Asia, many eat it for breakfast, lunch, and dinner.

• Rice is easy to digest, so it is one of the first foods given to babies.

• Rice Krispies are made from rice that has been popped – a bit like popcorn.

When rice is cooked it can be **fluffy** or **sticky**.

short grain rice

brown rice

Brown rice still has its bran layer. It tastes nutty.

This type of rice is light and fluffy when cooked.

long grain rice

arborio short grain rice

Short grain rice is good to eat with chopsticks because the grains are soft and stick together.

A creamy rice, arborio is excellent at soaking up flavours.

Arancini

These rice balls with melted cheese centres are delicious. Serve with a ready-made tomato sauce or make your own (see below).

Cook

Makes 5 large balls

Tomato sauce
Heat 1 tbsp olive oil and cook 1 diced shallot and 1 crushed clove garlic. Add 400 g (14 oz) tin tomatoes, 1 tsp brown sugar, and 1 tbsp tomato ketchup. Cook for 15 minutes.

You will need:
1 tsp olive oil
1 tbsp diced onion
60 g (2 oz) risotto rice
250 ml (8 fl oz) chicken or vegetable stock
3 tbsp grated Parmesan
salt and pepper
150 g (5½ oz) mozzarella, cut into 5 x 1½ cm (¾ in) pieces
2 tbsp dried breadcrumbs
1 egg, beaten with a pinch of salt
oil, for frying

1 Heat the oil. Cook the onion. Add rice and stock. Simmer for 25 minutes until cooked, stirring often. Add 2 tbsp Parmesan, salt and pepper.

Squash

2 Cool then refrigerate the rice for 3 hours or until firm. Then break it up, divide it into 5 portions, and squash into balls.

Squidge

3 Make a hole in each ball and push in a piece of mozzarella. Squidge the rice around the cheese.

Dip

4 Mix the breadcrumbs with the remaining Parmesan. Dip the rice balls in the egg.

Roll

5 Roll the rice balls in the breadcrumb mix.

Coated!

When the balls are completely coated, fry them in oil for 5 minutes or until golden.

These are made with **risotto rice** *and stick together perfectly!*

runny **mozzarella middles**

Paella

Paella was first made in Spain and gets its name from the pan it was cooked in – a *paelera*. This is a *paella mixta*, using seafood and chicken.

You will need:

1 onion
½ red pepper
1 clove garlic
1 tbsp olive oil
1 tsp smoked paprika or
    ordinary paprika
200 g (7 oz) long grain rice
600 ml (20 fl oz) chicken stock
2 tbsp tomato puree
170 g (6 oz) cooked chicken
handful parsley leaves
60 g (2 oz) frozen peas
170 g (6 oz) cooked prawns

Cooking with garlic

Choose plump garlic, and peel off the papery covering before chopping or squeezing in a garlic crusher.

Squeeze

Cook

1 First finely chop the onion, dice the pepper, and crush the garlic.

2 Heat the oil in a large non-stick frying pan and cook the onion for 5 minutes until soft.

3 Then add the pepper, garlic, and paprika. Pour in the rice and cook everything for 3 minutes, stirring constantly.

Pour

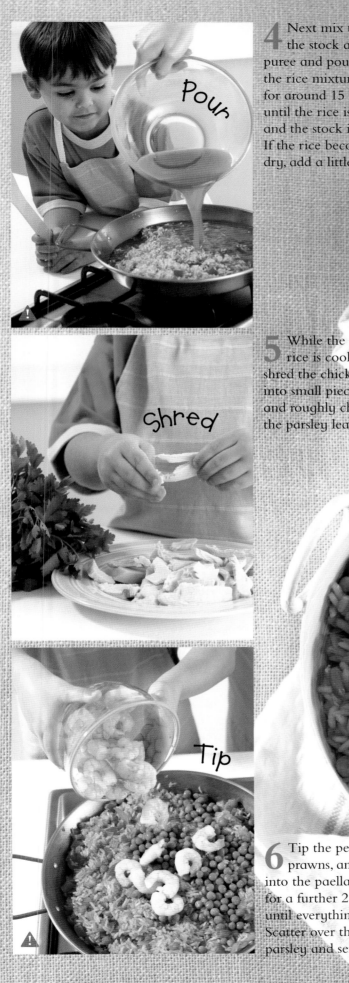

Pour

Shred

Tip

4 Next mix together the stock and tomato puree and pour this onto the rice mixture. Simmer for around 15 minutes until the rice is tender and the stock is absorbed. If the rice becomes too dry, add a little water.

5 While the rice is cooking, shred the chicken into small pieces and roughly chop the parsley leaves.

6 Tip the peas, prawns, and chicken into the paella and cook for a further 2 minutes, until everything is hot. Scatter over the chopped parsley and serve.

☆ **Annabel's Tip**
If you want an even more tomato-ey paella, try reducing the stock to 200 ml (7 fl oz) and adding a tin of chopped tomatoes with the other ingredients at step 4.

21

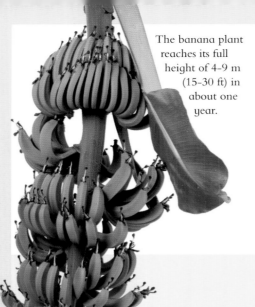

The banana plant reaches its full height of 4–9 m (15–30 ft) in about one year.

Each banana plant produces just one stem of fruit. Farmers cover it in plastic to stop insects laying their eggs in the fruit.

Bananas are harvested while they are still green. The heavy fruit is hung on cables so it can be moved around easily without bruising.

Bananas grow UPwards.

Bananas

This popular, peel-able fruit only grows in hot, tropical places. It is harvested all year round – so there are usually lots of bananas available in our supermarkets.

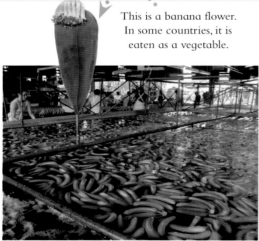

This is a banana flower. In some countries, it is eaten as a vegetable.

India is by far the largest producer of bananas in the world. There the banana flower is thought to bring good luck.

Monkeys like bananas too!

Some monkeys open bananas from the opposite end to us, pinching it with their fingers and tearing it open. Others eat the skin too!

types of bananas

baby banana

red banana

regular banana

plantain

At the factory, the bananas are cut into bunches of around 6–8 bananas. These are washed and cooled in big baths of water.

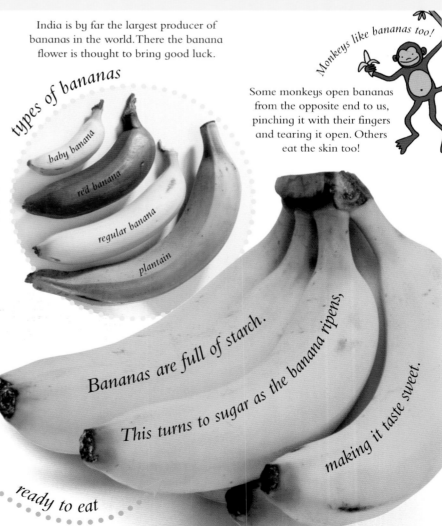

Bananas are full of starch.

This turns to sugar as the banana ripens,

making it taste sweet.

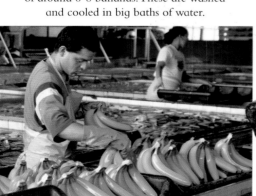

The bananas are checked for unwanted insects. They are weighed, labelled, packed in boxes, and sent to shops all around the world.

ready to eat

Banana Bites

This light pudding is fun for children to make. It works best with slightly under-ripe bananas.

Chop

Melt

Drizzle

Roll

You will need:
1-2 bananas
110 g (4 oz) chocolate –
milk or plain
desiccated coconut
sprinkles

Makes
6

1 Peel the banana and trim off the ends. Chop the flesh into 6 pieces.

2 Break the chocolate into a heatproof bowl. Put the bowl over a pan of warm water to melt the chocolate, stirring occasionally. Leave to cool slightly.

3 Push a straw through the banana, then drizzle melted chocolate over each piece. (Don't worry if it's not perfect – it still tastes delicious!)

4 Roll the chocolate-covered banana in the coconut or sprinkles. Let the chocolate harden, then serve.

chocolate sprinkles

coconut

coloured sprinkles

23

Banana Butterfly Cakes

These little cakes can be eaten plain, or covered in my sweet and sticky caramel topping – they'll be a flyaway success!

Makes 8

You will need:

For the cakes

1 large banana

110 g (4 oz) butter

110 g (4 oz) caster sugar

2 eggs

¾ tsp vanilla extract

110 g (4 oz) self-raising flour

For the icing

85 g (3 oz) cream cheese

40 g (1½ oz) unsalted butter

85 g (3 oz) Dulche de Leche

40 g (1½ oz) icing sugar, plus
   extra for dusting

☆**Annabel's Tip**
You can use any size nozzle to pipe the icing. I've used a fairly large one so the icing squeezes out easily.

☆**Annabel's Tip**
Dulche de Leche is a kind of caramel that you can buy in most supermarkets. It's a perfect ingredient for the caramel topping on these cakes.

Mash

Beat

1 First preheat the oven to 180°C/ 350°F/Gas 4. Line a muffin tin with 8 paper cases. Next peel and mash the banana and set it aside.

2 Put the butter and sugar in a large bowl and beat until pale and fluffy. In a separate bowl, beat together the eggs and vanilla. Then add the eggs to the butter mixture, a little at a time, beating thoroughly.

Sift

Fill

Beat

3 Now add the banana to the butter mixture and stir it in. Then sift the flour over the top and fold it in.

4 Fill the paper cases with the mixture. Bake for 20 minutes, or until risen and springy to the touch.

5 To make the icing, beat together the cream cheese and butter. Then beat in the Dulche de Leche and icing sugar.

Pipe

6 Slice the tops off the cakes and cut the tops in half to make butterfly wings. Pipe or spoon the icing onto each cake. Dust the wings with icing sugar, pop them on the cakes and serve.

☆Annabel's Tip
If you like, you can pipe a butterfly shape onto each cake using melted chocolate or writing icing.

25

Strawberries grow best in warm, sunny places. Farmers put straw under the plants to keep the fruit dry and protect it from rotting.

A strawberry flower has five white petals, and a bright yellow centre. This is where the strawberry fruit grows, as the petals fall away.

Strawberries only ripen when they are on the plant, so pick them when they are plump and red. If you pick them green, they stay green!

Strawberries

I love the beautiful red colour, melting texture, and sweet flavour of strawberries! They're a hugely popular fruit, and each year over two million tonnes of them are grown in gardens and fields around the world.

Farmers have found ways to grow the fruit all year long. This polytunnel works like a giant greenhouse. Sunlight gets in, but cold weather doesn't.

First comes the flower.

The petals fall off...

...as the fruit appears.

It gets bigger...

... and BIGGER.

Strawberries are the only fruit that have seeds on the outside.

Each strawberry has around 200 seeds.

Strawberry Layers

This is a super-easy recipe that can be used to make a rich layered pudding, breakfast treat, or around eight lovely ice lollies.

Hull

You will need:

350 g (12 oz) strawberries
4 tbsp strawberry jam
200 ml (7 fl oz) double cream
6 tbsp Greek yoghurt
mint, to serve

☆ **Annabel's Tip**
For delicious ice lollies, simply stir together the strawberry and cream mixtures, put in ice lolly moulds, and freeze.

Serves
6

Decorate with strawberries and mint.

1 Hull the strawberries. Put a few aside for decoration, and slice the rest into a bowl with the jam.

2 Use a potato masher to mash up the strawberries and jam.

Mash

3 In a separate bowl, whisk the cream to stiff peaks. Then fold the yoghurt into the cream.

4 Layer the strawberry and cream mixtures in little serving dishes.

Whisk

Strawberry Cheesecakes

These little cheesecakes are lovely made in heart-shaped tins, but the ingredients work just as well as one larger cheesecake, cut into slices.

Crush

Pour

Press

You will need:

sunflower oil, for greasing

170 g (6 oz) digestive biscuits

85 g (3 oz) butter

150 g (5½ oz) strawberries, plus
   extra to decorate

30 g (1 oz) sugar

2 tbsp water

135 g (4½ oz) packet strawberry jelly

200 g (7 oz) cream cheese

200 ml (7 fl oz) whipping cream

1 Grease your tins with sunflower oil. Put the biscuits in a bag and crush to fine crumbs using a rolling pin. Tip into a bowl. Melt the butter, pour it onto the biscuit crumbs, and mix thoroughly. Press into the bottoms of the tins.

Decorate with strawberries before serving.

☆ **Annabel's Tip**

To make one big cheesecake, use a loose-bottomed cake tin that's about 20 cm (8 in) across.

Chop

⚠

2 Next chop the strawberries into smallish pieces.

Slide

⚠

3 Slide them into a pan. Add the sugar and water and simmer until the strawberries are soft. Remove from the heat, add the jelly, and stir until smooth.

Pour

⚠

4 Leave the jelly mixture to cool. Whip the cream cheese. Pour the jelly mixture onto the cheese.

Whisk

5 Whisk to mix the jelly mixture and the cream cheese.

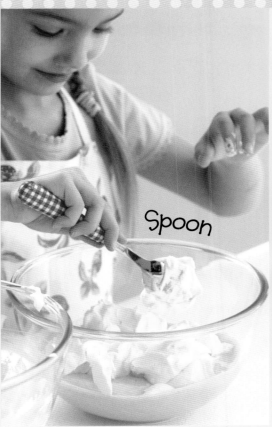

Spoon

6 Whisk the cream to stiff peaks. Spoon it onto the jelly and cream cheese and fold in. (It will start to set.)

Smooth

7 Spoon the creamy mixture onto the biscuits in the tins. Smooth the tops and refrigerate for 2 hours until set.

29

Apple trees in spring
This is when blossom grows on the trees. Flowers are pink, then gradually turn white. Bees pollinate the flowers so fruit can form.

Apple trees in summer
When the blossom falls, apples begin to grow in its place. They grow big and round and ripen in the sunshine.

Apple trees in autumn
The apples are ready! They are picked by hand so they don't get bruised. Then they are sent to shops and markets for sale.

Apples

Apples are a fantastic fruit as they are equally delicious in savoury and sweet dishes. They've been grown for around 4,000 years and are one of the oldest and best-loved fruits there is.

Pip, pip HOORAY!

There are all sorts of varieties of apples. Here are a few of them.

There are nearly 10,000 different kinds of apples.

Apple trees can keep on producing fruit for over 100 years.

The country that produces the most apples each year is China.

Royal Gala

Bramley

Golden Delicious

Braeburn

Red Delicious

Temtation

Pink Lady

Much of an apple's goodness is just under the skin, so don't peel it before you eat it!

To stop a cut apple turning brown, sprinkle it with lemon juice.

About a quarter of an apple is air. That's why it floats!

Baked Apples

Eating or cooking apples are equally good in this super-simple recipe. It's delicious served with my sauce suggestion below, or with a lovely big blob of yoghurt!

You will need:
4 apples
6 tbsp raisins
3 tbsp brown sugar
¼ tsp cinnamon
15 g (½ oz) butter
6 tbsp water

 Core

 Stuff

 Pour

1 Preheat the oven to 180°C/350°F/ Gas 4. Remove the cores from the apples using an apple corer. Then put the apples in a baking dish.

2 Mix together the raisins, brown sugar, and cinnamon. Stuff this mixture into the holes in the apples. Top with the butter.

3 Pour about 6 tbsp water around the apples so it just covers the bottom of the dish. Bake for 35–40 minutes, basting halfway through cooking.

Serves 4

*Before cooking, **score** around the apples so they don't **burst open**.*

☆Annabel's Tip
For a quick-and-easy treat, serve each apple with 1 tbsp Dulche de Leche mixed with a little cream.

Apple Meringue Tarts

These simple little apple tarts topped with meringue are lovely eaten warm or cold. Serve them with vanilla yoghurt or cream.

The meringue should be soft on the inside...

...and slightly crisp on the outside.

You will need:

For the tarts
200 g (7 oz) ready-rolled shortcrust pastry
2–3 apples
2 tbsp water
15 g (½ oz) caster sugar
1 tsp lemon juice

For the meringue
1 large egg white
40 g (1½ oz) caster sugar

☆**Annabel's Tip**
If you are using a block of shortcrust pastry, or rerolling trimmings, you'll only need about 110 g (4 oz).

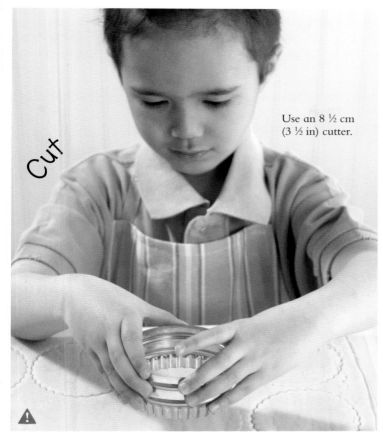

Cut

Use an 8 ½ cm (3 ½ in) cutter.

1 Preheat the oven to 200°C/400°F/Gas 6. Cut 6 circles from the pastry and use these to line a muffin tin.

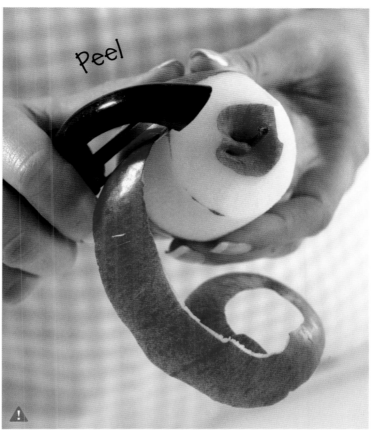

Peel

2 Peel, chop, and cook the apples in the water until soft and fairly dry. Stir in the sugar and lemon juice.

Spoon

3 Let the apples cool a little then mash them into small pieces. Spoon into the pastry cases and bake in the oven for 15 minutes.

Whisk

4 For the meringue, whisk the egg to stiff peaks. Whisk in 1 tbsp sugar, then whisk in the remaining sugar. Pipe or spoon onto the apple and cook for a further 3–5 minutes.

Apple & Chicken Curry

This mildly spicy curry is made with ingredients you can buy at your local supermarket. The apple adds a lovely sweetness to the dish.

You will need:

1 onion
1 clove garlic
3 spring onions
1 medium apple
1 tbsp vegetable oil
1-2 tsp mild curry paste
1 tsp soy sauce
150 ml (5½ fl oz) coconut milk
1 chicken stock cube, dissolved in
    150 ml (5½ fl oz) boiling water
5 cm (2 in) piece lemongrass
2 chicken breasts, cubed
110 g (4 oz) frozen peas
salt and pepper
coriander, sliced lime, and boiled
    jasmine rice, to serve

Serves 4

1 First prepare your vegetables and fruit: peel and chop the onion, crush the garlic. Thinly slice the spring onions. Cut the apple into thin slices.

Cut

Pour

☆ Annabel's Tip
To shape your jasmine rice into a star, grease a star-shaped mould with sunflower oil. Spoon cooked rice into the mould. Push it down. Then carefully slip off the mould.

2 Heat the oil in a wok. Add the onion and cook for 5-6 minutes until soft. Add the garlic and curry paste and cook for 1 minute. Then pour in the soy sauce, coconut milk, and chicken stock, stirring constantly.

Add apples

Add peas

3 Add the lemongrass, chicken, and apple. Bring the curry to a boil, then reduce the heat and simmer for 6–8 minutes until the chicken has cooked through.

4 Add the peas and spring onions and cook for a further 1–2 minutes. Season to taste with salt (the soy sauce is salty so be careful) and pepper.

jasmine rice

slice of apple

5 Remove the lemongrass and spoon the curry onto plates. Serve with a sprinkling of coriander, a few slices of lime, and boiled rice.

35

People keep honeybees in wooden hives so the honey can be collected easily. Fifty thousand bees can live in each hive. These are worker bees, drone bees, and just one queen bee.

Here honey is being scraped off honeycomb. But honeycomb can also be put into a machine that spins very fast so that the honey flies out. Then the honey is put in jars.

Bees make honey from a sweet liquid, called nectar, which they suck out of flowers. Many flowers have bright colours to help bees find the nectar.

When the honey is ready, bee keepers puff smoke into the hives to make the bees sleepy. Then they pull the honeycombs out of the hives. Honeycombs contain the honey.

Honey

Bees make honey to feed themselves during the winter. But they often produce more than they need, so people collect the extra and use it to add a touch of sweetness to all kinds of recipes.

Dip a honey spoon in honey and twirl it round. It picks up lots of honey and drips less than an ordinary spoon.

buzz

Bees fill honeycomb with honey, then cover it over with wax until the honey is needed.

Bees live in hives and in the wild. This nest of wild bees is in Thailand.

Honey can be creamy yellow, golden, or amber.

• Workers are female bees. Each worker makes around ½ tsp honey in its lifetime.

• The drones are male bees. They fertilize the eggs the queen bee lays.

• The queen is the only bee that can have babies.

You can eat honeycomb like this. Not all honey tastes the same. The flavour comes from the flowers the bees feed on.

Honey-glazed Salmon

Here I've used honey and soy sauce to make a type of glaze called teriyaki. It's delicious on salmon.

Add

You will need:

4 tbsp clear honey
4 tsp soy sauce
2 tsp rice wine vinegar
¼ tsp grated ginger
170 g (6 oz) skinless salmon fillet, cut into cubes
1 tsp water

Decorate with curls of spring onion.

Serves 4

First soak 6 wooden skewers in warm water for 30 minutes. Heat the grill to high.

1 Mix together the honey, soy sauce, and vinegar. Pour half into a pan and set aside. Add ginger to the remaining mixture in the bowl.

Pour

2 Pour the ginger mixture onto the salmon. Mix to coat.

3 Thread the salmon onto the skewers, then put them on a foil-lined baking sheet.

Spoon on sauce from the bowl. Grill the salmon for 2–3 minutes on each side or until cooked. Add the water to the sauce in the pan. Simmer for 30 seconds, then serve with the salmon.

Thread

Ready to grill

☆**Annabel's Tip**
To make the onions curl, cut them into thin slices and put them in icy-cold water.

Honey Cakes

Although these little cakes are sweet enough to eat on their own, children love making bees and flowers to decorate them. So help them get busy!

You will need:

For the cakes
60 g (2 oz) salted butter
60 g (2 oz) soft light brown sugar
4 tbsp clear honey
1 egg
½ tsp vanilla extract
2 tbsp apple puree
85 g (3 oz) self-raising flour
½ tsp ground cinnamon
¼ tsp ground ginger

For the bees and flowers
200 g (7 oz) marzipan
melted chocolate or writing icing
12 flaked almonds
sprinkles

Pour

Makes 6

1 Preheat the oven to 180°C/350°F/ Gas 4. Line a muffin tin with 6 paper muffin cases. Put the butter and sugar in a mixing bowl. Pour in the honey and beat everything together until fluffy.

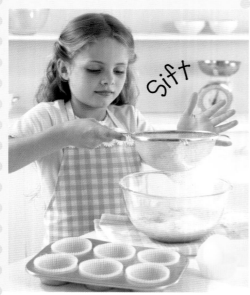

Sift

2 In another bowl, beat the egg, vanilla, and apple puree, then beat this into the butter mixture. Sift over the flour, cinnamon, and ginger.

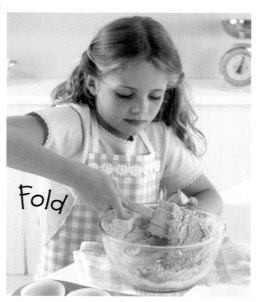

Fold

3 Now fold in the dry ingredients by running your spatula around the outside of the bowl and across the middle until everything is well mixed.

Fill

4 Fill the paper cases with the mixture. Bake for 18-22 minutes, until risen, golden, and firm to the touch. Leave to cool on a wire rack.

38

Shape

Paint

☆ **Annabel's Tip**
For nut-free decorations, make the bees with yellow-fondant-icing bodies and chocolate-button wings.

5 To make the bees, shape the heads and bodies from marzipan and gently squash them together so they stick. Cut out flower shapes.

6 Paint on the bees' faces and stripes using melted chocolate or writing icing. Push flaked almonds into the sides for wings. Press sprinkles into the flowers.

Cut out the flowers using a small cookie cutter.

I've got my stripes!

Decorate your cakes with bees and flowers.

cocoa pod

cocoa beans

white pulp

Cocoa pods grow on the trunk and main branches of a cacoa tree. When the pods are split open, you can see the cocoa beans inside.

Cocoa pods grow to the size of melons. Workers cut them from the trees when they are ripe-yellow to dark-red colour.

Chocolate

Sweet, creamy, and rich, chocolate is one of my favourite cooking ingredients! It is made from cocoa beans, the seeds of the cacao tree that grow in tropical rainforests.

cocoa beans

cocoa mass

cocoa butter

Chocolate melts at just below body temperature – that's why it turns to liquid so quickly when you hold it in your hand.

Swiss people eat more chocolate per head than any other nation on Earth.

PLAIN CHOCOLATE is cocoa mass mixed with sugar and cocoa butter.

MILK CHOCOLATE has the same ingredients as plain chocolate, but also contains milk.

WHITE CHOCOLATE only contains cocoa butter – not cocoa mass. That's why some people don't think it's really chocolate at all.

• Here a worker is spreading out wet cocoa beans to dry in the sun.

• Then they're sent to a factory where the shells are removed, leaving the insides called *nibs*.

• The nibs are roasted, ground, and pressed to separate them into *cocoa mass* and *cocoa butter*.

• The cocoa mass is melted and mixed with sugar and some of the cocoa butter. It's poured into moulds and hardened into the chocolate bars we buy in shops.

Chocolate Truffles

Home-made chocolate truffles make delicious gifts. For a special present, sit a couple of truffles on a piece of card, wrap in plastic, and tie with ribbon.

You will need:
100 g (4 oz) bar of plain or milk chocolate
3 tbsp double cream
½ tsp vanilla extract
15 g (½ oz) butter
2 tbsp cocoa powder
2 tbsp coconut

Snap

Stir

Roll

1 Snap the chocolate into a bowl. Add the cream, vanilla, and butter. Put the bowl over a pan of simmering water to melt the chocolate, stirring occasionally.

2 Let the chocolate mixture cool, then put it in the freezer. Stir every 5 minutes or so until the mixture is thick and fudgy.

3 For each truffle, roll a teaspoon of the fudge mixture into a ball in your hands (quickly so it doesn't melt). Then roll it in cocoa powder or coconut.

☆ **Annabel's Tip**
Lay the truffles on baking parchment and store in the fridge for up to a week – if they last that long!

a delicious treat

Makes 12–15

Dark and White Chocolate Puddings

These rich chocolate puddings hide a surprise — as you cut into them, white chocolate comes flowing out! Serve on special occasions.

You will need:

110 g (4 oz) butter, plus extra
  for greasing
150 g (5½ oz) plain chocolate
1 whole egg
2 egg yolks
3 tbsp caster sugar
½ tsp vanilla extract
1 tbsp cornflour
3 white chocolate truffles
vanilla ice-cream, to serve

☆ Annabel's Tip
You can use ordinary white chocolate instead of the truffles. Use 2 squares of chocolate in each pudding, and cook for at least 14 minutes to give the white chocolate a chance to melt.

1 Preheat oven to 190°C/375°F/ Gas 5. Generously butter 3 mini metal pudding basins and line the bases with baking parchment.

Snap

2 Snap the chocolate into a heatproof bowl. Add the butter and put the bowl over a saucepan of warm water so the chocolate and butter melt, stirring occasionally. Set aside to cool slightly.

Beat

Pour

Place

3 Put the egg, yolks, sugar, and vanilla in a bowl. Using an electric mixer on high, beat them together for 4–6 minutes until pale and about 4 times the original volume.

4 Pour the chocolate mixture into the egg mixture. Add the cornflour and whisk everything together to make a batter.

5 Spoon 2 tbsp of the batter into each mould and place one truffle in each. Cover the truffles with the remaining batter.

6 Put the moulds on a baking sheet and bake for 10–12 minutes until just set on the surface. Leave for 2 minutes, then turn out onto plates and serve straight away with vanilla ice-cream.

Sweet treasure hidden here...

Most yoghurt is made from cows' milk. Friendly bacteria in the milk make it thicken and take on a tangy, yoghurty flavour.
One cow produces enough milk in a day to make more than 100 little pots of yoghurt.

Yoghurt

Yoghurt is made from milk. Although you can buy it in supermarkets, it is actually very easy to make yourself. And you can use any milk you like – full-fat, half-fat, skimmed, goat's milk, sheep's milk – they all work!

• Yoghurt was first eaten over 2,000 years ago. It was probably discovered accidentally when milk was left out in the sun.

• Yoghurt is a good source of calcium, so will help build strong bones and teeth.

• Some yoghurt contains living bacteria that can help you digest your food.

Lots of yoghurt has added sugar – this sweetens the flavour and helps the yoghurt last.

Homemade yoghurt

1 First boil 1L (2 pt) milk to kill unwanted bacteria. Let it cool.

2 Then add a pot of plain, live yoghurt to the milk and stir it in.

3 Keep the mixture warm (around 43°C/110°F). You can either put it on a radiator, or in a very low oven for 6 hours or overnight.

4 The mixture will thicken and turn to yoghurt. You can eat this plain (although it is rather sharp), or add fruit and honey. Enjoy!

☆Annabel's Tip
Look out for frozen yoghurt in the ice-cream section of your supermarket It's delicious on chopped-up banana or a bowl of berries.

Fruit Brûlée

Yoghurt makes a perfect topping for a fruit brulee. *Brûlée* means "burnt" in French, but really the sugar is grilled until it has just melted.

Serves 4

You will need:
200 g (7 oz) strawberries
110 g (4 oz) blueberries
3 tbsp icing sugar
120 ml (4½ fl oz) double cream
200 g (7 oz) Greek yoghurt
½ tsp vanilla extract
2 tbsp demerara sugar

Dust

Whisk

Spoon

1 Hull and quarter the strawberries and put them into a bowl with the blueberries. Dust over 1 tbsp of the icing sugar and toss to coat the berries.

2 Whisk the cream to soft peaks. In a separate bowl, mix together the yoghurt, vanilla, and remaining icing sugar. Fold the cream into the yoghurt.

3 Spoon the berries into 4 ramekins and put the yoghurt mixture on top.

Try using other fruits too.

4 Sprinkle on the demerara sugar, then pop the brûlées in the freezer for 15 minutes. Heat the grill to high. Grill as close as possible to the heat until the sugar has melted.

Cool slightly before serving so the sugar forms a crisp crust.

Chicken Pittas with Yoghurt & Mint Dressing

This is a mildly spicy dish with a lovely cooling minty dressing. Serve in pitta breads for a light lunch or supper.

You will need:

For the chicken
4 tbsp natural yoghurt
1 tsp mild curry paste
1 tsp clear honey
1 tsp lemon juice
8 chicken mini fillets

For the dressing
4 tbsp natural yoghurt
1 tsp lemon juice
pinch of salt
8 mint leaves

To serve
4 small pitta breads
1 little gem lettuce

Makes
4

Serve while the chicken is still warm.

☆ **Annabel's Tip**
Make sure you wash your hands after handling raw chicken. And check that it is cooked all the way through before serving.

Mix

1 First put the yoghurt, curry paste, honey, and lemon juice in a bowl and mix together. Add the chicken and mix to coat. Cover and leave to marinate for 30 minutes (or overnight in the fridge).

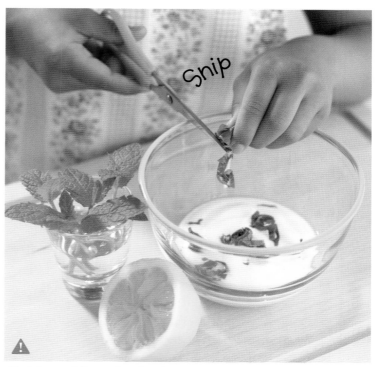

Snip

2 Meanwhile make the dressing: put the yoghurt, lemon juice, and salt into a bowl. Roll the mint leaves into a cylinder and use scissors to snip into little ribbons. Mix everything together and keep in the fridge until needed.

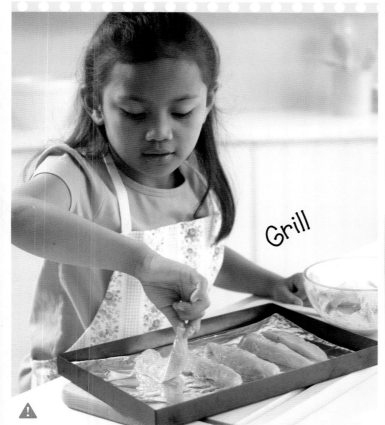

Grill

3 Preheat the grill to low. Put the chicken on a lined baking sheet. Spoon over half the marinade left in the bowl and grill for 6 minutes. Turn the chicken over, spoon on the remaining marinade, and grill for 6 minutes or until cooked.

Fill

4 Warm the pittas under the grill so they puff up. As soon as they are cool enough to handle, split them open and fill with the lettuce leaves, chicken, and yoghurt dressing. Then serve.

Index

Annabel Karmel

Annabel is a leading author on cooking for children and has written more than 25 best-selling books that are sold all over the world.

She is an expert in devising tasty and nutritious meals for children without the need to spend hours in the kitchen.

Annabel writes for many newspapers and magazines and appears frequently on radio and TV as one of the UK's experts on children's nutritional needs. She has her own range of healthy foods for children in supermarkets.

Annabel was awarded an MBE in the 2006 Queen's Honours List for her outstanding work in the field of child nutrition.

Other children's titles written by Annabel
Children's First Cookbook 978-1-4053-0843-4
Mummy and Me Cookbook 978-1-40532-880-7

Visit Annabel's website at
www.annabelkarmel.com

Acknowledgments

With thanks from Annabel to: Valerie Berry, Rachael Foster, Dave King, Mary Ling, and Caroline Stearns for their help in making this book. **And thanks to the children who appeared in the photographs:** Ruby Christian-Muldoon, Luella Disley, Sonny Edwards, Meganne Galivo, Lewis Matton, Ethan Michaels, Dominic Mosca, Samuel Phelps-Jones, Molly Saunders, Jaden Stauch, Chloe Tingle, James Watson, Brian Wong, and Natalya Wright. **Thanks also to:** Katie Giovanni and Seiko Hatfield.

Picture Credits: The publisher would like to thank the following for their kind permission to reproduce their photographs:
(Key: a-above; b-below/bottom; c-centre; f-far; l-left; r-right; t-top)
Alamy Images: Balfour Studios 30ftl; Ricardo Beliel / BrazilPhotos 40tr; Blickwinkel / Schmidbauer 4fbr; Adam Burton 44t; Nigel Cattlin 14tr, 30tl; Central America 22bl, 22tr; Dennis Cox 18tr; Foodfolio 5bl, 36fbr; Andrew Fox 26cl; Paolo Gallo 10fcra; Mark Gibson 30tr; Greenshoots Communications 40tl; Tim Hill / Cephas Picture Library 5ftl; Wayne Hutchinson 14tl; James Clarke Images 10t; Dennis MacDonald 36tl; Ian McKinnell 18tc; Photography 1st 22tc; Ingo Schulz / Imagebroker 36fbl; Martin Shields 22clb; Jason Smalley / Wildscape 36ftl; Eric Tormey 30ftr; Maximilian Weinzierl 4bl; Andrew Woodley 4fbl; Russell Young / Danita Delimont 36tr. **Corbis**: Ted Horowitz 36fclb. **Getty Images**: DAJ 26tc; Johner Images 6tc; Nordic Photos / Jerker Andersson 36ftr; Photographer's Choice / Ian O'Leary 26tr; Science Faction / Ed Darack 6tl; StockFood Creative / Lew Robertson 36bc; Tim Graham Photo Library 14tc; Win-Initiative 6tr. **Photolibrary**: 40tc; Digital Vision / Akira Kaede 18tl. **StockFood.com**: Susie M. Eising 40br; Bernd Euler 40fcl; FoodPhotogr. Eising 26tl; Studio Schiermann 22cb.
All other images © Dorling Kindersley. For further information see: **www.dkimages.com**